Walt Disney's

WINNIE-THE-POOH
Picture Dictionary

A GOLDEN BOOK, NEW YORK
Western Publishing Company, Inc.
Racine, Wisconsin 53404

A

acorns

Piglet is gathering *acorns*.

airplane

The *airplane* flies high in the air.

apple

The *apple* is red and round.

asleep

Eeyore is *asleep*.

B

banana

Christopher Robin
is eating
a *banana*.

bed

Roo's *bed* is soft
and warm.

bicycle

Can you ride a *bicycle*?

boots

Piglet has
shiny new *boots*.

breakfast

For *breakfast* Pooh
is having cereal
with honey.

C

camp

Pooh and Piglet are setting up *camp*.

carrot

A *carrot* is a crunchy vegetable.

chair

Very Small Beetle sits in a cozy *chair*.

clock

A *clock* tells us what time it is.

custard

Roo's favorite food is *custard*.

daisy

Tigger picks a *daisy*.

desk

Owl sits at his *desk*.

draw

He likes to *draw* pictures.

drum

Christopher Robin beats the *drum*.

E

earmuffs

Tigger has new *earmuffs.*

eat

Pooh loves to *eat.*

elephant

Roo has a toy *elephant.*

empty

The honey pot is *empty.*

fan

A *fan* can make us cooler.

fish

Roo has caught a *fish*.

flashlight

Rabbit's *flashlight* shines on the path.

Hi!

friends

Pooh and Piglet are best *friends*.

G

glass

Roo drinks his juice from a *glass*.

gloves

Christopher Robin wears *gloves* on cold days.

grapes

Grapes grow in bunches.

grasshopper

A *grasshopper* is an insect that jumps.

guess

Guess who is hiding behind the tree.

hat

Tigger has a new *hat*.

helicopter

Christopher Robin has fun playing with his toy *helicopter*.

hide

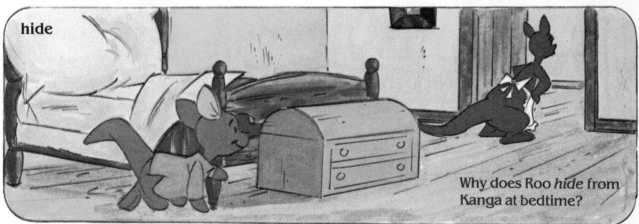

Why does Roo *hide* from Kanga at bedtime?

house

This *house* is Piglet's.

TRESPASSERS WILL

ice

Tigger skates on the *ice*.

icicles

See the *icicles* on the roof.

iron

Kanga presses Roo's shirt with an *iron*.

ivy

Very Small Beetle got lost in the *ivy*.

jacket

A *jacket* is a short coat.

jelly

Roo likes lots of *jelly* on his toast.

juggler

Have you ever seen a *juggler*?

jump

Piglet tries to *jump* over the puddle.

Oops!

K

kettle

Kanga boils water in a *kettle*.

key

The *key* to Pooh's honey cupboard is in a safe place.

kick

Will Owl *kick* the ball back to Tigger?

kite

On windy days, Piglet flies his *kite*.

knee

Christopher Robin hurt his *knee*.

ladder

Piglet climbs the *ladder*.

lamp

Owl has a *lamp* for reading.

leaf

Very Small Beetle got lost under a *leaf*.

lemonade

Lemonade is good to drink on a hot day.

lunch

For *lunch,* Pooh is having honey and butter sandwiches.

M

marbles

Piglet and Roo are playing with *marbles*.

mirror

Eeyore looks at himself in the *mirror*.

mittens

Tigger has new *mittens*.

moon

The *moon* is full and bright.

mud

It is fun to make *mud* pies.

nail

Tigger hits the *nail* on the head!

nap

Eeyore is taking a *nap*.

nest

Have you ever found a bird's *nest*?

numbers

Do you know all the *numbers*?

0123456789

oatmeal

Pooh pours honey over his *oatmeal*.

onion

Rabbit is slicing an *onion*.

open

The oven door is *open*.

oven

A cake is baking in the *oven*.

paint

Piglet is going to *paint* the birdhouse.

pajamas

Roo has new *pajamas*.

peach

A *peach* is sweet and juicy.

pillow

Tigger and Roo are having a *pillow* fight.

Q

quiet
It is *quiet* time for Rabbit's friends-and-relations.

quilt
They are covered up with a *quilt*.

R

raincoat
Piglet has a new *raincoat*.

record
Kanga plays her favorite *record*.

rose
A *rose* smells sweet.

sailboat

Very Small Beetle has a *sailboat*.

sandwich

A peanut butter *sandwich* is good to eat.

seesaw

Pooh and Piglet are on a *seesaw*.

supper

For *supper,* Pooh is having more honey and butter sandwiches!

sweater

Tigger has a new *sweater*.

tent

On their camp-out, Pooh and Piglet are going to sleep in a *tent*.

toothbrush

Pooh brought his *toothbrush*.

train

Christopher Robin plays with his toy *train*.

turtle

The *turtle* has a hard shell.

umbrella

Piglet has a new *umbrella*.

under

Very Small Beetle is *under* the umbrella.

vase

A *vase*
is for flowers.

violets

Pooh likes *violets*.

visit

Tigger has come
to *visit* Eeyore.

W

wagon

Pooh has a *wagon* filled with honeypots.

window

Christopher Robin's *window* is open.

write

Owl can *write* his ABC's.

worm

A *worm* does not have any legs.

xylophone

Roo plays the *xylophone*.

yarn

Sweaters are made from *yarn*.

yawn

Do you *yawn*
when you are tired?
Eeyore yawns a lot!

yo-yo

Tigger is playing with a *yo-yo*.

zebra

Christopher Robin plays with his toy *zebra*.

zipper

The jacket has a *zipper*.

Do you know all the words in this book from acorns to zipper?